T0085409

Accent on
GILLOCK

by William Gillock

CONTENTS

ISBN 978-0-87718-079-1

EXCLUSIVELY DISTRIBUTED BY

WILLIS MUSIC

HAL•LEONARD®

Visit Hal Leonard Online at
www.halleonard.com

World headquarters, contact:
Hal Leonard
7777 West Bluemound Road
Milwaukee, WI 53213
Email: info@halleonard.com

In Europe, contact:
Hal Leonard Europe Limited
42 Wigmore Street
Marylebone, London, W1U 2RY
Email: info@halleonardeurope.com

In Australia, contact:
Hal Leonard Australia Pty. Ltd.
4 Lentara Court
Cheltenham, Victoria, 3192 Australia
Email: info@halleonard.com.au

At the Ballet

William Gillock

Tempo di menuetto

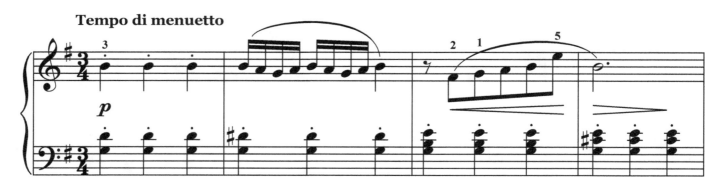

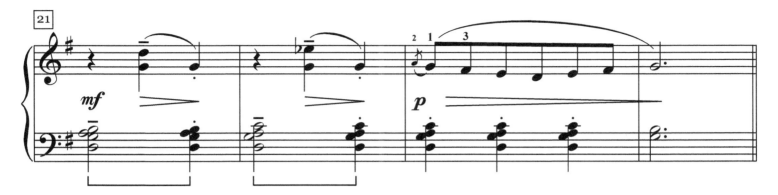

Capriccietto

William Gillock

Allegretto

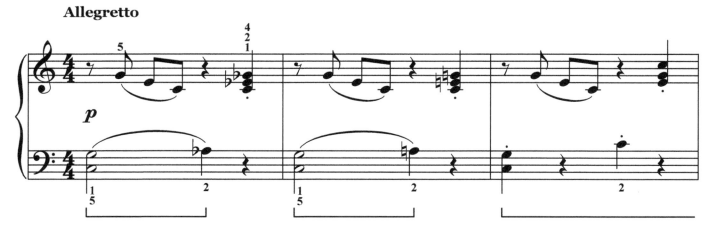

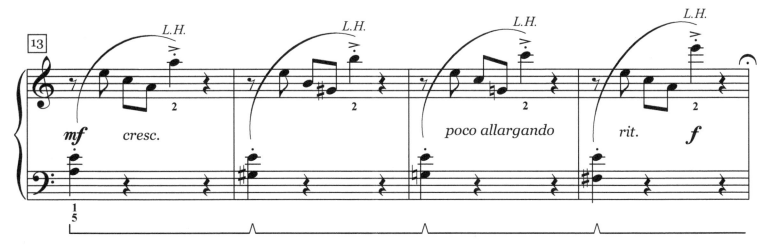

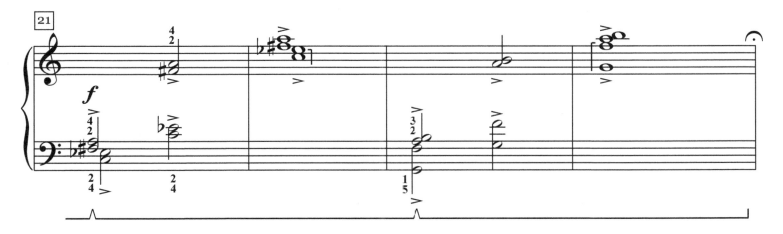

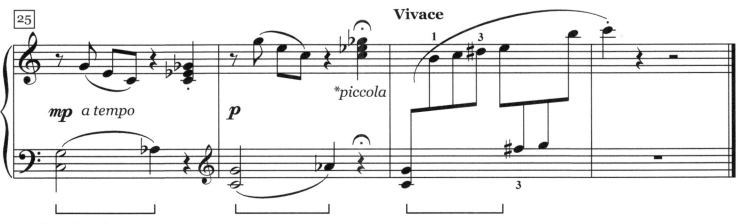

* Italian for "short"

Fiesta

William Gillock

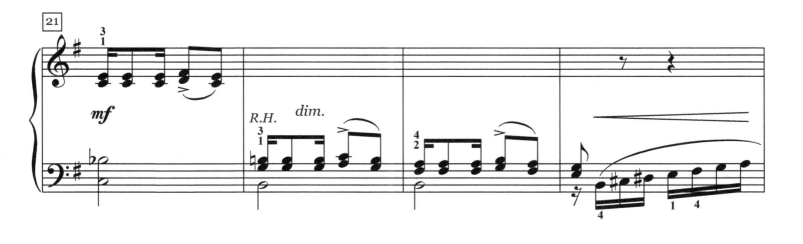

D.C. al Fine

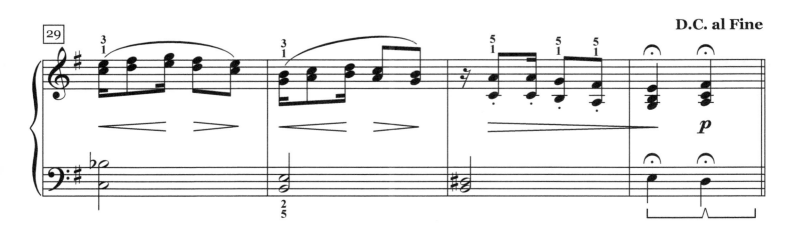

Harlequin

To Attica

William Gillock

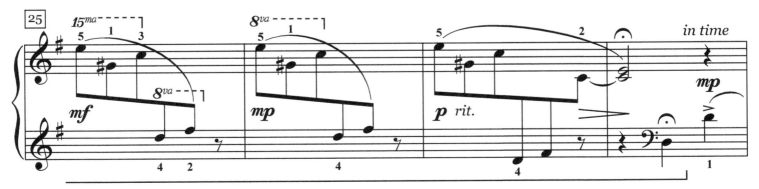

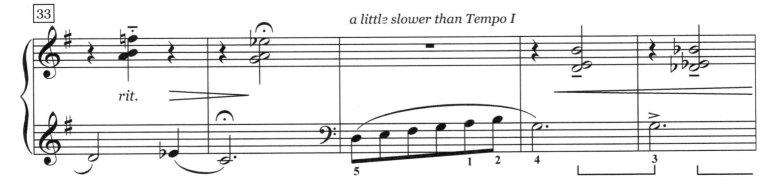

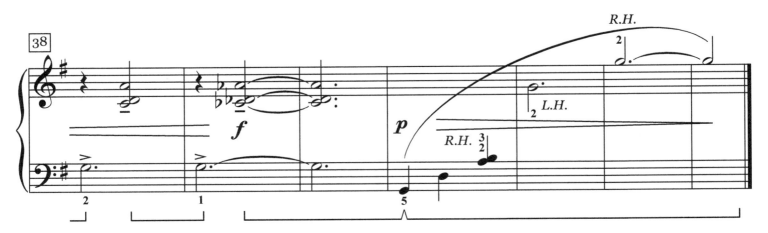

Last Spring

William Gillock

Largo, con poco moto

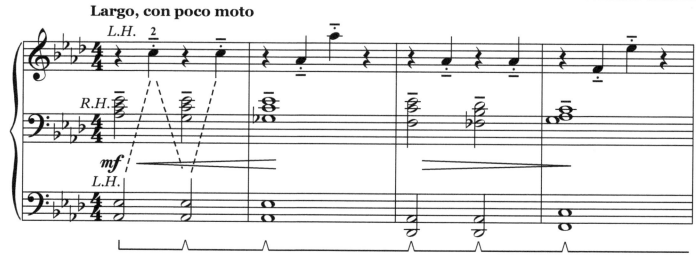

Più mosso

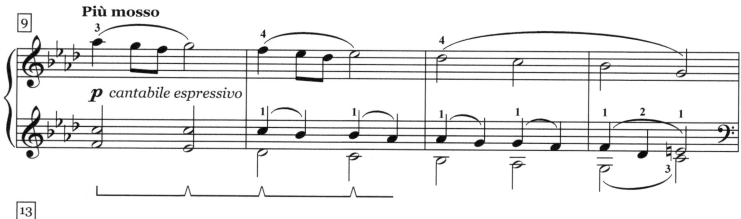

Tempo I

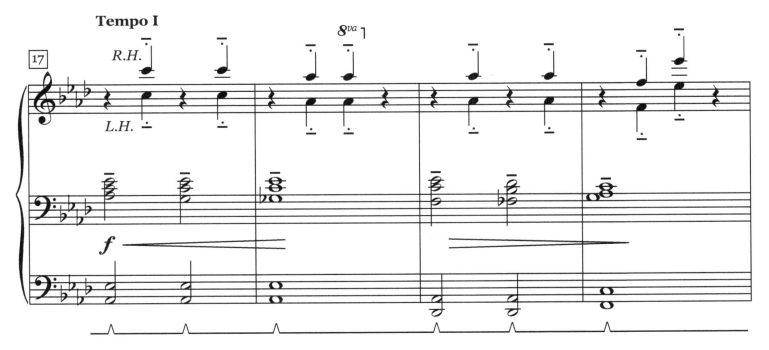

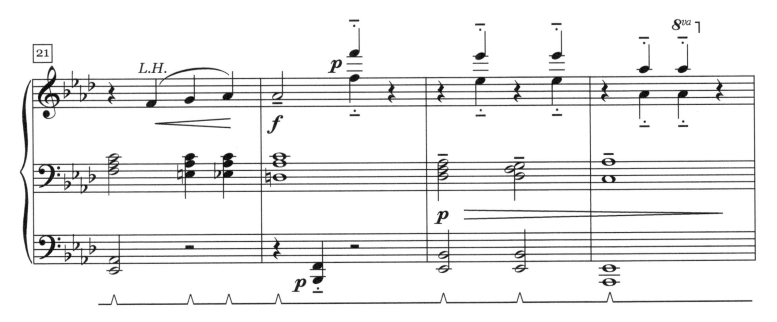

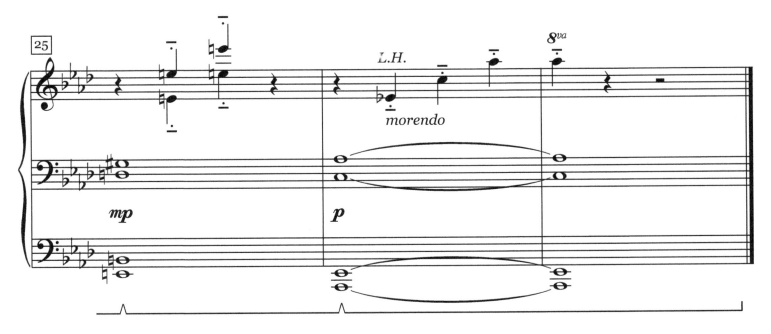

Old Homestead

William Gillock

Adagio espressivo

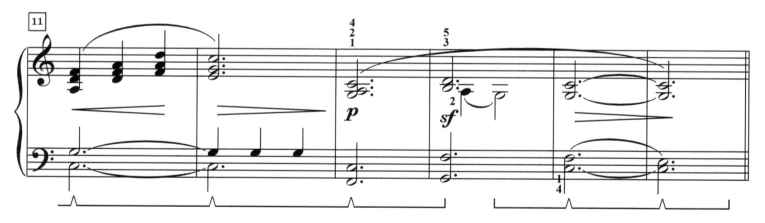

Poco più mosso

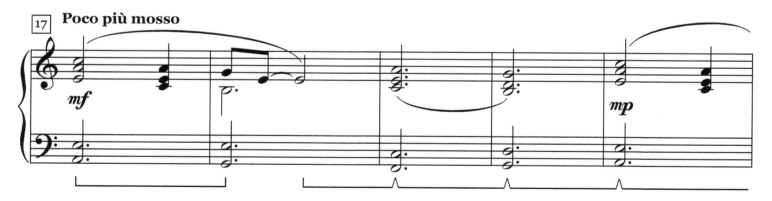

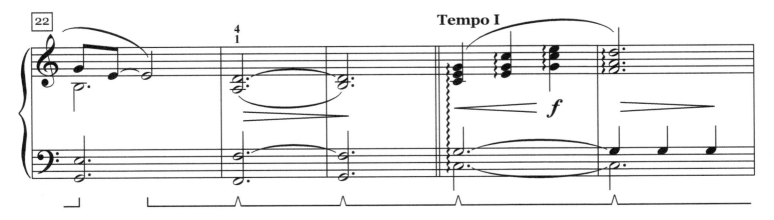

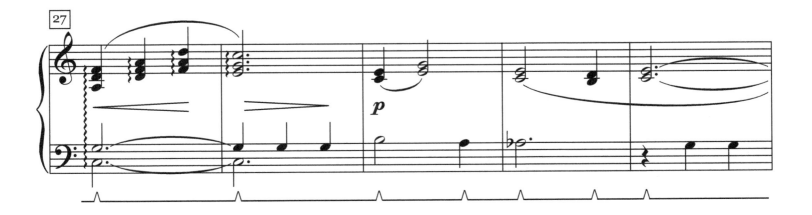

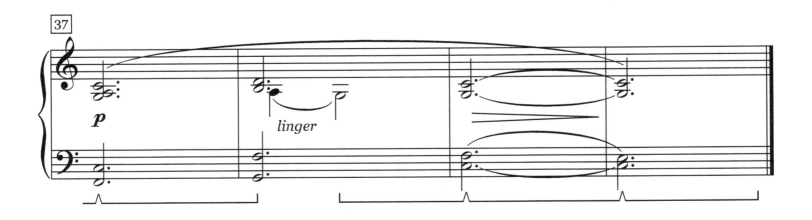

To Ruth Baskett
Lazy Bayou

William Gillock

Gently drifting ♩ = c. 66

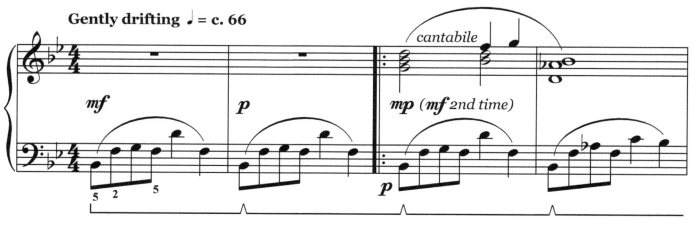

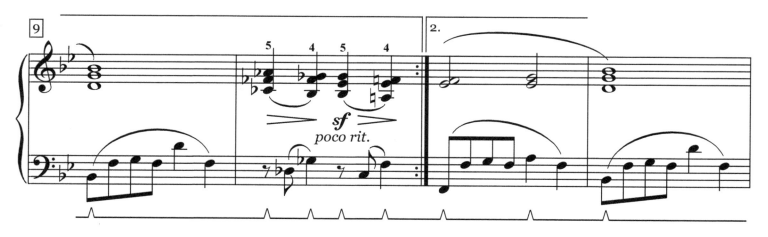

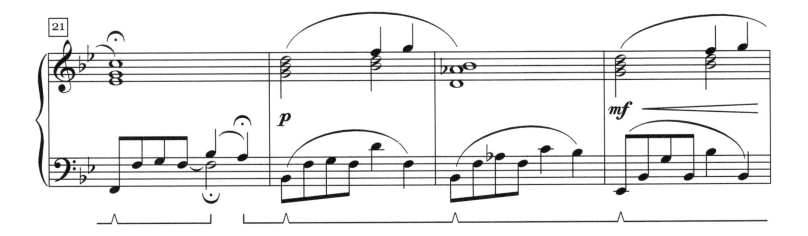

Also available:

ACCENT ON GILLOCK: COMPLETE
All Eight Volumes in One
00361225